Cindy and Jimmy Pot
3202 Thursh Lane
Rolling Meadows Ill.

SKY PIONEERS

WEEKLY READER CHILDREN'S BOOK CLUB

Presents

Sky Pioneers

The Story of Wilbur and Orville Wright

JEANNE LeMONNIER GARDNER

Illustrated by Douglas Gorsline

HARCOURT, BRACE & WORLD, INC., NEW YORK

For my mother and father

SKY PIONEERS

ONE

Wilbur Wright walked swiftly along the path leading to the schoolhouse. His younger brother, Orville, lagged behind, zigzagging back and forth to crunch autumn leaves with his feet. It was a September morning in the year 1876 in the city of Dayton, Ohio.

"Hurry up, Orv! We'll be late!" Wilbur said as his long legs kept their steady marching pace. Wilbur was nine, four years older than his brother.

Orville had stopped to watch a long-wingéd swallow fly into the green-gold maple trees. "Wouldn't it be fun if we could fly to school?" he said dreamily.

Wilbur slowed his steps. His sandy brows drew together in a frown. "I wonder how it would feel to fly," he said.

Just as Orville caught up with Wilbur, they heard someone call their names. "Orv! Will! Come here a minute. I want to show you something." Orville's friend, Ed Sines, was calling from the door of the Sines's barn. Orville ran toward Ed.

"You'll be late," Wilbur warned him.

"I'll catch up," Orville said over his shoulder.

Ed led the way into the barn. "Look," he said, "my mother's old sewing machine. She put it out here because it's broken."

Orville liked machines better than anything in the world. "Maybe we can *fix* it!" he said. His blue eyes shone with excitement. "Once I helped my mother oil her sewing machine. I'll show you how it works."

Ed watched wide-eyed as Orville explained the machine. The time grew later and later. Suddenly Ed said, "Orv, won't your mother scold you for not going to school?"

Orville gasped with surprise. "Oh! . . . I hadn't meant to stay so long. I wonder what my teacher will say!" A worried look crossed his face. Then his eyes gleamed with mischief. "I know what I'll do," he said. "I'll wait until school is over. Then I'll go home. Maybe Mother won't know."

"I wish I were old enough to go to school," Ed said. "Is it fun?"

"Sometimes," Orville said. "You'll find out when you go next year."

The boys tinkered with the machine all morning. They put drops of water in the oil holes. Orville attached a wire to the foot pedal.

"If we can make it work, let's sew a tent," Ed said.

Orville nodded. "Sails for a boat, too." Orville had gone sailing with his father once. He remembered how much he had liked gliding across the water. As he worked on the sewing machine, he forgot his worries about school.

On his way home later Orville worried again about staying away from school. He knew it was wrong. He wondered if he should tell his parents.

The house was quiet when he got home. "Were you late this morning?" asked Wilbur, looking up from a book. Wilbur was always reading. It was his favorite hobby.

"I have a secret," Orville said. "Promise not to tell? I didn't go to school."

"You're going to catch it!" Wilbur said.

"Well, I was trying to fix a machine. Father says we should learn by *trying*."

"But you can't learn *everything* from tinkering," Wilbur said.

At supper that evening, Orville was not hungry.

"What's the matter, son?" asked Father. "Don't you feel well?"

Orville looked across the table at Wilbur. Then he looked at Father. He swallowed hard. "I played hooky, sir," he said.

"Can I play hooky, too?" asked their little sister, Katharine.

"Hooky means staying away from school," Wilbur said.

Orville told the family about trying to fix the sewing machine. "It was so much fun that I forgot everything else," he said. "But I won't stay away from school again."

Father and Mother smiled at each other. "It's good that you have told us, Orv," Father said. "Truth is always the best. And we're glad you understand that school is important."

Orville was happy his secret was out. Suddenly he was hungry.

TWO

The Wright family lived in a plain white-shingled house on Hawthorne Street. There was no running water in the house. There was no electricity either. But that was not unusual in 1876.

The boys pumped water from a well in the back yard. They carried the water into the kitchen in pails. They chopped logs piled in the woodshed to burn in the big cookstove. They helped their mother fill the oil lamps.

Mother helped the boys, too. She helped them with their hobbies, and she helped them learn to use wood-working tools. "You must always measure carefully," she told them whenever they wanted to make something. She showed them how to make drawings for models and experiments. Mrs. Wright's father had been a wagonmaker. "How happy I was when he allowed me to help him!" she told her sons. Now she shared her knowledge with her children. Once she helped them to make a sled. It was the fastest sled in the neighborhood. Often she turned one of their broken toys into a new and different plaything. The family was proud of her cleverness. Orville and Wilbur's friends liked to play at their home because Mrs. Wright never scolded if their hobbies and games made a mess in her kitchen.

Mr. Wright was a minister and the editor of a church newspaper. He often went to other cities on church business. One time he brought home with him a special present for the boys. He held it hidden in his hands while they tried to guess what it could be.

"Now watch closely, boys!" Father said. When he opened his hands, the mystery present whirred up toward the ceiling. It hovered in the air a second or two, then dropped to the ground.

"What is it, Father?" Wilbur asked as he ran to pick it up.

"It's a flying machine!" Orville said excitedly.

"Whoever heard of a flying machine?" said his older brother scornfully. "There's no such thing!"

"Even so," said Father, "that's a good name for it."

The small toy was made of thin strips of bamboo covered with tissue paper. There were wings at each end held in place with rubber bands. The boys had never seen anything like it before.

"What makes it fly?" Wilbur asked.

Father showed them how to twist the rubber bands to wind it. They all took turns.

Even little Katharine had a turn. "Be careful, Katharine," Orville said. "Hold it gently or you will squash it."

It was not a strong toy. The boys had to glue it together many times. Orville liked fixing it as much as he liked flying it. At last it was too badly broken to be fixed any more.

"We'll make a new one," Wilbur said.

This was fun. They measured the broken strips of wood and cut new pieces the same size. They cut pieces of tissue paper and glued them to the thin sticks to make the wings. When they had finished, the new flying toy looked almost like the broken one. They were proud that it worked.

"Let's make a bigger one," Orville suggested later.

"Yes," Wilbur agreed, "and after that we'll make one still bigger. We'll keep on making them bigger and bigger and bigger until we make one big enough to ride on."

After days of trying, the boys gave up. Only a very small model like the one Father had brought them would work.

As they grew older, the brothers went on doing things together. Every year they had new ideas for things to make.

When Orville was ten, he wanted to make a kite. "Will you help me?" he asked his brother.

Wilbur, who was fourteen, felt too grown up for kites, but he agreed to help his younger brother. They worked together all morning. After lunch they took the kite for a test.

"The wind is strong," Wilbur said. He held the kite high, waiting to toss it into the air.

"Oh! Let me! Let me!" Orville said.

Orville ran down a hill with the kite.

"Faster!" Wilbur shouted. "Let out more string!"

A gust of wind caught the kite, and it began to rise. Then suddenly it dove to the ground—broken and torn.

"Oh, Will! Look at our kite," Orville said. "It's wrecked!"

"Never mind. We'll make a better one tomorrow," Wilbur promised. "I have a new idea."

Wilbur bent the frame of the new kite to a greater curve.

"This way it should hold more wind," he said. When they took it for a test, other boys were there flying kites.

"What a funny-looking kite the Wrights have!" teased the boys. "It's crooked!"

But soon they stopped teasing. The new kite flew higher than all the others. It stayed up longer, too.

"Hey, Orv," yelled one of the boys, "will you make me one like it?"

"Me, too?" asked another. All the boys wanted one.

Still guiding the kite aloft, Orville moved nearer to where Wilbur was standing. "We'll make them," he said to his friends with excited pride, Then, with a mischievous smile at Wilbur, he added, "Ten cents each, and that's only *half* the store price!"

As the boys watched their kite glide high in the sky, Orville said with a sigh, "I wish we could be up there, too."

"Maybe some day we can," Wilbur answered.

THREE

Selling kites was only one way to earn money. Orville collected scrap metal in his wagon and sold it at the junk yard. He raked leaves and shoveled snow for neighbors. Once he and his friends gave a circus and sold tickets.

Wilbur had a job folding newspapers. The work was easy—too easy for him. "There must be a better way to do a simple job like this," he thought to himself as he folded page after page with his strong, slim hands. The more he thought about it, the more determined he became to find a way to speed the work. Soon he began spending his spare time at home inventing a paper-folding machine. It grew into a strange-looking object with wooden rollers, strings and gears, and a foot pedal to supply the power. It was big, bulky, noisy. It worked.

When he was a senior in high school, Wilbur was hurt seriously in an ice-hockey game. He had to stay in bed for many months. At first he was not even allowed to read. His illness prevented his going to college that fall. This was a bitter disappointment to him. Unlike Orville, who usually did his homework in a hurry in order to have time for hobbies, Wilbur enjoyed the hours he spent studying and reading. He had looked forward to going to college.

Orville worked extra hard during his brother's long illness. He did his own chores, and he did Wilbur's too. Often he read to Wilbur. As the months passed, Orville began to talk excitedly about a new hobby.

"I'm going to be a printer," Orville said. "I've been reading about printing, and I've been practicing on a toy press Ed Sines has. Some day I am going to have a real one."

One evening Mr. Wright talked to Wilbur about Orville's new hobby. "Orv's in love with the printing business," Father said, "and I would like to surprise him."

"How, Father?" Wilbur asked.

"Do you remember the little boat we made together several years ago?"

Wilbur looked puzzled. "Yes," he said, "I remember it. It's still out in the woodshed. But it leaks, and it's not worth fixing."

"Well," Father went on, "if you have no plans for it, I know a man who wants it for its lumber. He will trade us a printing press for it. It's only a very small press, but it's real."

"That's a fine idea, Father," Wilbur said. "A good trade, too! Orv will be surprised all right!"

Orville could hardly believe his eyes when Father brought home the printing press. He spent every spare minute working with it. Mother let him use an empty room upstairs. Soon Orville and Ed Sines began printing a small newspaper, which they sold to their eighth-grade classmates.

Because he wanted to learn more about the business, Orville worked in a printing shop during the next two summer vacations. He built another press at home. When he was nearly seventeen, he experimented making a larger one. It was much harder than he had thought it would be. Wilbur offered to help. Although some of his ideas were unusual and different, they worked!

"Where do you get such strange ideas?" Orville asked him.

Wilbur grinned at his younger brother. "I get most of them

from *you!*" he said with a look of merriment in his blue-gray eyes.

The boys worked together as partners publishing a neighborhood newspaper, which they named *The West Side News*. Wilbur was the editor. Orville was the printer.

Running a weekly paper was a man-sized job. They gathered news items and sold advertisements to local businessmen. Wilbur wrote most of the stories. He discovered that he liked writing almost as much as he liked reading. Orville set the type and ran the press. Puttering with the machinery was the part he liked best about the newspaper business.

The people of Dayton liked *The West Side News*. Orville and Wilbur kept the paper going for over a year. During that time Orville finished his high-school studies.

"I'm not going to college," he told his family. "I'd rather work with Will in the print shop."

Mrs. Wright died that year. She had been proud of her sons. Orville and Wilbur always remembered the encouragement she had given them in each of their efforts. The memory of her faith was to help them all their lives.

FOUR

Automobiles were unknown to the people of Dayton in 1892. When they could not walk from one place to another, they rode in trains or trolley cars or in horse-drawn carriages. Some rode old-fashioned high-wheeled bicycles.

A new kind of bicycle became popular later that year. Its two wheels were the same size. People called it "the safety."

Orville bought one of the new bikes. "Why don't you get one, Wilbur? We could go places together."

"I could go, too," their sister Katharine said. "Many ladies are riding bikes nowadays. That's why the fashions are changing. Haven't you noticed how much shorter we are wearing our skirts—almost above our ankles?"

"Yes, I've noticed," Wilbur said. "And I notice many men are riding bikes to their shops and offices. It seems as if *everyone* in Dayton is riding bikes."

In fact, people all over the United States were pedaling bicycles over the streets and dusty roads. City people rode their bikes to the country for picnics. Country folk rode to the cities to see plays at the theaters and to dine in the restaurants. Young and old—men and women, boys and girls—all rode bikes. Races were popular, too.

Orville practiced for the bike races. He found that he could ride faster by leaning low over the handlebars. He told Wilbur about it.

"That's because the wind skims over the curve of your back. It cuts down the wind resistance," Wilbur explained. "Let's try raising the seats and lowering the handlebars on our bikes. That way we can ride faster into the wind without getting tired."

"What on earth have you done to your bike, Orv?" asked one of the other riders at the starting line of the races one Saturday. "You look silly bent over so far."

"Wait and see!" Orville yelled as the whistle blew. The racers started out pedaling as fast as their legs would move. Orville kept pace with the rest of them. Halfway around the track some of the riders began to lag behind. As they grew tired, more and more of the riders were forced to slow their pace. Orville won the race easily. As the other boys reached the finish line, tired and puffing, they looked again at Orville's bike. He told them about wind resistance. Some of them asked him to change their bikes that way, too.

"Sure," Orville said. "Bring them to the print shop tomorrow. Will and I can fix them."

It wasn't long before Wilbur and Orville were as busy fixing bicycles as they were running the printing shop.

"Why don't we open a bike repair shop?" Orville suggested one day.

"We might as well," Wilbur said. "We're spending almost as much time working on bikes as we are on the newspaper. We could sell bicycles, too."

So they rented a small shop and hung out a large sign, *Wright Cycle Company*. Now there were two stores in Dayton

with the Wrights' name. Ed Sines was hired to run the printing shop for them.

As the months went by, more and more people bought bicycles. The Wrights sold them, and they fixed them when they were broken.

One afternoon Wilbur grumbled, "Orv, there isn't space enough in this shop for another bike!"

Orville nodded in agreement. "We haven't enough time any more for our work at the print shop." A look of mischief shone in Orville's eyes. "Ed will buy our printing business if we want to sell it," he said. "I'm willing, if you are."

"I figured you'd feel that way. Printing is too easy for you now that the press doesn't need so much fixing," Wilbur teased.

The printing business was soon sold to Ed Sines, and the Wright Cycle Company was moved to a larger shop. The brothers believed that they could make a better bicycle than those they were already selling. Soon they began to manufacture a bike of their own design. They called it the *Van Cleve*. Besides being less expensive than other models, the Van Cleve had special safety brakes.

Behind the shop the brothers built a shed for experiments. "These old wheels should be good for something," Orville said one morning, pointing to a pile of old bike parts stacked in a corner. "I have an idea for some fun."

Using old parts and some pipe, they made a bicycle with two seats and two sets of pedals and handlebars. It was called a *tandem*.

"I declare," said one of their neighbors, laughing. "Look at Orv and Will Wright whiz down the street on that two-seater bike! You never know what those boys will invent next!"

FIVE

"Listen to this," Wilbur said one evening while reading a newspaper by the gas lamp in the parlor. "It says that a man in Germany—his name is Lilienthal—has made some kind of *glider* to fly on. It's made of light wood covered with cloth. I'd sure like to see it."

"I'd like to *try* it!" Orville answered. "What fun that would be!"

"It sounds dangerous to me," Katharine added softly, looking up from her sewing.

Orville and Wilbur were interested in any new invention. They often borrowed books from the public library in order to learn more about science and engineering. They wanted to know what made every new invention work. After reading about Mr. Lilienthal's glider, they read all they could find about flying in books and magazines.

They found out that the idea of flying had been in the minds of men for centuries. Inventors and dreamers had tried to fly.

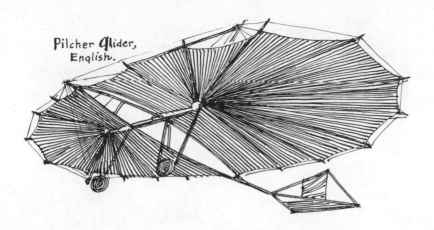

Pilcher Glider,
English.

Some had fastened large wings to their arms and jumped from steep hillsides or rooftops. Most of these had been seriously injured or killed.

Orville and Wilbur felt a sharp sadness when they later read that Mr. Lilienthal had crashed and died trying to fly his glider. "I wonder what went wrong," Wilbur said. After that he and Orville talked more and more about flying. They read and studied what other scientists and inventors had tried. They learned that most of these men had given up, saying firmly that flying was impossible.

"*We* could build a glider, Will," Orville said. "I know we could."

"It would be fun to try, but it might cost a lot of money," Wilbur said. "Those others who have tried had plenty of money for buying materials."

Chanute's Glider.

"Maybe that's *why* some of them failed," Orville argued. "Maybe they were in a hurry to build their machines, knowing they had money enough to keep on trying if they failed."

"Perhaps," Wilbur said, "but I'd need to know much more about wind currents and air pressure before I'd be willing to build a glider. I wonder what we could learn from watching the birds."

At sunrise for the next few Sundays Wilbur and Orville rode three miles on their bikes to a spot along the Miami River called The Pinnacles. Here, where the river waters rush over jagged rocks, they lay on the grassy shore, squinting into the bright morning sunlight. Buzzards and hawks soared among the towering rocks, seeking food near the shallow rapids.

"Watch that one!" Wilbur said, pointing to a diving hawk. "Notice how he glides without seeming to move his wings?"

"I wish we knew his secret," Orville said.

The boys knew that a glider had to balance or it would crash. This was the problem that had caused other inventors to fail. It was this same problem that had caused Lilienthal's fatal crash. Without balance control, a glider was at the mercy of the wind. Some inventors had tried hinging wings to a frame. Others had tried to balance by shifting their bodies from side to side. Some others had even tried feather-covered wings tied to their arms. None of these methods had worked.

The more Orville and Wilbur thought about balancing and controlling a glider, the more challenging the problem became. They talked about it, and they argued about it. Sometimes Wilbur would convince Orville of a way to obtain balance, only to end up arguing against his original idea.

Late one evening, while Wilbur was working alone at the bike shop, a customer came in. "I'm glad you're still open," the man said. "I need an inner tube for this wheel."

Wilbur took a tube from a long box and handed it to the man. The customer inspected the tube. While waiting, Wilbur

twisted the empty box in his hands. A strange feeling puzzled
him.

Wilbur stared at the box. He twisted it again. Suddenly he
saw what had puzzled him. It was not a problem at all. It was
the answer to one! The angle of the twisted box showed him an

answer to wing balance for a glider. The idea is now called
"wing warp."

Wilbur was so excited with his discovery that he hurried
the customer out of the shop impolitely. He could hardly wait
to get home and share his discovery with Orville.

Orville was as excited as his brother. "You've done it, Will!" he said. "This *is* the answer! One end of the wing can be raised and the other lowered to keep the wind from upsetting the glider. *Now* we can make one!"

"Not so fast!" Wilbur said. "First we will have to make a giant kite to see if the idea works."

A group of small boys followed Wilbur when he took the huge kite for a test. They were curious, and they wondered why a grown man would want to fly a kite. Wilbur was thirty-two now, and his sandy hair was beginning to thin on top of his head.

"Gee, Mr. Wright, that sure is a big kite! Why does it have two wings and all those wires?" asked one of the boys.

Wilbur liked children. "It's an experiment," he said. "Let's see if it will fly."

Afterward Wilbur decided to tease Orville, who had stayed to tend the bike shop. Wilbur drooped his shoulders and walked into the shop, pretending to be sad and discouraged. He did not say a word.

Orville glanced at his brother and quickly clasped his hands together. "*Now* we can build our glider!" he said. "It worked!"

"How did you know?" Wilbur asked with surprise.

"It's easy," Orville said. "You forgot to wipe the grin off your face."

SIX

The shed behind the bike shop was busier than ever now. Wilbur and Orville often worked late at night building the glider.

"Riding on this will be the best of all sports!" Orville said anxiously. "Where shall we test it?"

Wilbur scratched his thinning hair. He thought a moment. "We need a place where the wind is strong and steady—"

"—a place without trees," Orville broke in.

"Yes—with sandy ground for soft landings," Wilbur added. "I'll write to the United States Weather Bureau. They can tell us."

The answer from the Weather Bureau named several windy places. The nearest one was a fishing village on an Atlantic Coast island off North Carolina. It was called Kitty Hawk.

Wilbur wrote a letter to the weather station there to find out more about Kitty Hawk. The postmaster, William Tate, answered that it was: "a stretch of sandy land one mile by five with a bare hill in center 80 feet high, not a tree or bush anywhere to break the evenness of the wind current."

This made the Wrights sure that Kitty Hawk was the best place for testing their glider. They packed the glider parts into big crates. Wilbur started off early in September, 1900. Orville stayed behind to finish work at the bike shop.

"I'll meet you at Kitty Hawk as soon as you have a camp ready!" Orville called as the train pulled out of the Dayton station.

When Wilbur got off the train at Elizabeth City, North Carolina, he asked a man where to get the boat for Kitty Hawk.

"Kitty Hawk? Never heard of it!" the man answered.

SEVEN

Wilbur was disappointed to find that he had missed by one day the weekly boat to Kitty Hawk.

At the waterfront he met an old sea captain, Israel Perry, who owned a dirty flat-bottomed schooner.

"So you want to go to Kitty Hawk, eh?" Captain Perry said. "That's a lonely place—nothing there but a weather station and a post office. Well, climb aboard and stow your gear. I'll take you."

Wilbur looked thoughtfully over the choppy waters toward Albemarle Sound. Then he stared long and hard at the battered boat tied up at the wharf. "It doesn't look safe," he thought. "But I can't waste six days waiting for the regular boat. I'll take a chance."

By afternoon, the howling winds had lashed the water to white foam. The leaky boat tossed and smacked in the rough waves of the Sound.

"We'll have to head into the North River until it quiets

down," Captain Perry finally shouted over the noise of the storm. After they had anchored in the quiet river waters, the captain said, "Let's have something to eat while we wait this out."

Wilbur smacked his lips and followed the captain to the schooner's small galley. He was hungry. Then as they entered the crowded cooking area, his stomach turned upside down. Everything was dirty and greasy.

"No thanks, Captain," Wilbur gulped politely. "I'm not hungry."

When they finally landed at Kitty Hawk, Wilbur went directly to the home of the postmaster, William Tate.

"Land sakes!" said Mrs. Tate when she learned that Wilbur had spent two days on the boat with nothing to eat. "That's only a short trip on the regular boat. You must be starved!" In a few minutes she set before Wilbur a steaming plate of ham and eggs.

"Thank you, Mrs. Tate. This is mighty kind of you," Wilbur said. He told Mr. and Mrs. Tate about the glider. They liked him. He was well-mannered and thoughtful. But flying was a *crazy* idea! Could such a sensible young man be *serious* about it?

Wilbur stayed with the Tates until he had finished setting up camp. He dragged supplies half a mile over the wind-swept sands. He pitched the tent at a spot where a few trees gave shade from the hot sun. It was hard work hauling the crates of tools and glider parts. His muscles were sore from carrying water and food supplies.

"I thought camping was supposed to be fun," he groaned as he slapped at a pesky mosquito.

After Orville arrived they worked together assembling the

glider. Wilbur borrowed Mrs. Tate's sewing machine. He stitched yards and yards of white sateen for the wing coverings.

When they had finished putting it together, the glider looked like a big box kite with wings. It weighed fifty-two pounds and had cost about fifteen dollars to make.

At first Orville and Wilbur flew the glider as if it were a kite, controlling it with long ropes. In gusty winds it bobbed wildly like a bucking bronco.

"You're not really going to try to *ride* on that thing, are you?" Mr. Tate asked them.

"That's why we came to Kitty Hawk, Mr. Tate," Orville said. "Tomorrow we're going over to Kill Devil Hill to try it without the ropes."

Next day the Wrights carried the glider four miles over the

sand to the highest hill on the island. Mr. Tate went along to help.

"This is the real test, Will," Orville said as they made ready for the first glide.

From the top of the sandy dune the brothers took turns alone. Because the glider remained close to the soft, sandy hillside, there was little chance of a serious crash, but the speed of their flights was about twenty miles an hour—fast traveling for the year 1900. The glider stayed in the air only a few seconds on each of these downhill flights before one wing would touch the ground and force them to land. It could scarcely be called flying. But these experiments gave Orville and Wilbur a chance to test their ideas of balance. It was exciting to ride on their big flying kite, even though the rides were short and close to the earth.

"It doesn't stay up as long as we had hoped it would," Orville said after they had taken turns making several trips.

"But we can balance it in the air," Wilbur said. "No one else has been able to do that before."

"I didn't expect that thing to hold you up for a split second," said Mr. Tate. "I am surprised that you even got it off the ground."

"We'll think of a way to keep it up longer," Wilbur said. "We'll be back next year."

EIGHT

At home again in Dayton, Wilbur and Orville plunged into plans for a new glider. Wilbur wrote a letter to a famous engineer, telling about their glider experiments. This man was Octave Chanute. He was interested in flying, too, and he had written a book telling about the flying experiments of inventors all over the world. Wilbur and Orville had read and studied Mr. Chanute's book. They had disagreed with all the ideas it told about. But they thought Mr. Chanute might be interested in their experiments.

In July, 1901, the brothers went back to Kitty Hawk with a larger glider. This time they built a wooden shed to shelter it. Mr. Chanute came to their camp to see the experiments.

Although the new glider flew longer distances than the first one, Orville and Wilbur were disappointed with it. It did not have the lifting power they had expected.

During one of Wilbur's rides the glider stalled in the air. "Watch out!" Orville screamed from below. His warning alerted Wilbur to the danger. This was how Mr. Lilienthal had crashed! Orville held his breath while Wilbur inched his weight forward to level the machine. Then he turned the rudder control and steered the glider to a safe landing.

"That was a narrow escape," Orville said, "but it proves that our control system works."

Even though these experiments had set new distance records for gliding, both brothers were discouraged. Until now they had thought of flying as a hobby. The trips to Kitty Hawk had been their vacations. The experiments had been sporting and fun.

Now the fun was over. Gliding with the wind was only a first step. What they really wanted to do was fly without regard to the wind. There would be many problems to solve. The fun would change to hard work and long hours of study.

One of the most important problems to be studied was air pressure. Older scientists had made charts of air pressures. The charts were printed in science books and were used by teachers and scientists in many experiments. Orville and Wilbur were sure that these charts were wrong. But how could they prove it?

Mr. Chanute told them to keep trying. "You have already set new gliding records," he said. "Your experiments are more promising than any others."

As they were packing to go back to Dayton, Wilbur said in a discouraged voice, "I don't think man will fly for a thousand years."

But Wilbur and Orville did not give up. Every day after they had finished work at the bike shop, they checked over notes and charts they had made of their glider tests. They began to trust their own ideas more than ever.

That fall Wilbur was invited by Mr. Chanute to speak in Chicago at a meeting of engineers. Wilbur was terrified by the idea. "I'm only a bicycle mechanic, Orv. I'd feel silly making a speech before all those college men."

"You can't disappoint Mr. Chanute," Orville said.

"All right," Wilbur agreed at last. "But I'm going to tell those engineers that we think the air pressure figures in the textbooks are wrong."

That worried Orville. "Maybe Will and I are mistaken," he thought to himself. "Maybe those old charts are right after all. It would make us look silly if we were wrong."

Orville went to work on an idea and devised a small wind tunnel to measure air pressure. He had time for only a few tests, but it was time enough to prove that the textbooks held mistakes. Later he and Wilbur made a better wind tunnel. Then, after many experiments, they made careful notes telling exactly how much air pressure was needed to lift surfaces curved at different angles. Now there was no question about the old measurements. They were wrong, and Orville and Wilbur were

right! No wonder no one had ever before been successful with
flight trials.

Late in August, 1902, Orville and Wilbur went to Kitty
Hawk again. Now they had a new glider. Its measurements were
based on the new air-pressure figures they had discovered
through their wind-tunnel experiments. By the time their "vaca-
tion" was over, they had made almost a thousand flights. The
long hours of practice had made them good glider pilots. They
had made important changes to improve the glider's balance
and control. No longer did it wobble or nose-dive. Now they
were satisfied with it.

"All it needs is a motor," Wilbur said.

"Let's get back to the bike shop and earn the money to come
back next year," Orville said. "Our glider is ready for a motor,
and we are ready to fly!"

NINE

In 1903 most people thought flying was a fool's dream. They made fun of automobiles then, too, and called them "rich men's toys."

Except for Katharine and Father, only one other person in Dayton knew of the brothers' flying experiments during their Kitty Hawk vacations. This was Charlie Taylor, chief mechanic at the bike shop.

When Orville and Wilbur could not find the right kind of motor for their glider, it was Charlie who suggested, "Why not make one?"

With Charlie's help, an engine was planned and made. Finally, after many arguments, the brothers agreed on a design for propellers.

Late in September they returned to Kitty Hawk. First they repaired storm damage to their camp. They made the shed larger so they had enough space inside for cooking and for sleeping. It took them another three weeks to assemble their six-hundred-pound flying machine. In between times, they made practice flights on their 1902 glider.

There were many problems. The propeller shafts broke off when they first started the motor, and they had to make new ones. The plane's wings had to be made stronger. The weather was bad.

"Will we *ever* be ready for a test?" Orville asked impatiently.

"We must be sure of *everything*," Wilbur said.

Orville knew his brother was right. They had worked so hard and so long. Riding a strange new machine into the air was dangerous. A man could be killed if it failed.

On December 14 everything was ready at last. A coin was tossed to see who would have first chance. Wilbur won the toss

and climbed into the pilot's position, flat on his stomach, on the bottom wing. The motor roared and shook as he guided the plane down the greased wooden track built for the take-off. The machine began to rise slightly into the air, but it nosed into the soft sand three seconds later.

"Are you all right, Will?" Orville called anxiously.

"I'm all right," Wilbur answered, "but I'm afraid part of the machine is wrecked."

The brothers were too honest to call this a successful test. They were disappointed, but they were not discouraged. They could fix the machine and try again.

Three days later—December 17, 1903—they were ready for another try. The wind was tricky and cold. Icy puddles dotted the sand. "I wish we had warmer clothes," Wilbur said as he hugged his overcoat to his sides. Three men from the weather station came over to watch and to help. Mr. W. C.

Brinkley turned up from a neighboring village, and so did seventeen-year-old Johnny Moore, who had nothing better to do that day.

It was Orville's turn to try. He warmed up the motor. Then he climbed into position. Carefully he unhooked the wire that held the machine to the starting track. The noisy machine started forward very slowly.

Wilbur ran along beside the machine, holding the wing tip to steady it. It began to go faster and rose into the air a few inches. It rose higher and then dipped toward the ground. Orville's heart pounded as he worked the controls to bring the nose up. Within seconds he was about ten feet off the ground. Tense and anxious, Wilbur and the others watched.

Orville did not have time to think about being afraid. He was busier than he had ever been before. Both of his hands and both of his feet were busy working the controls. For twelve seconds he kept the wobbly machine in the air against a gusty wind. Then he landed it safely.

The flight was short, but that did not matter. What counted was that the machine had lifted from level ground and traveled through the air under its own power for a distance of 120 feet! For hundreds of years men had dreamed of flying. And now, two young men—bicycle mechanics from Ohio—had conquered the air!

After it was over, Orville and Wilbur proudly shook hands. It was a solemn moment. Then they grinned at each other and laughed and jumped up and down like small boys. They slapped each other on the back and talked excitedly at the same time.

"We did it, Orv!" Wilbur shouted. "We really did it!"

"I didn't have time to think about it in the air," Orville said. "But I'd have frozen to death if I hadn't been so busy."

"Too bad Will Tate wasn't here to see it," said Mr. Brinkley. "He kept telling us you boys weren't crackpots. He said you were real scientific. Guess maybe he was right."

TEN

Aviation history began that wintry December 17.

Wilbur and Orville made three more flights that morning. On the last test Wilbur flew a distance of over 800 feet. The plane stayed up for 59 seconds against a strong wind.

That afternoon they hiked four miles to the weather station to telegraph the good news to Father. "Inform press," their wire ended.

But the newspapers—even the Dayton *Journal*—paid no attention to the story. Only one editor understood how important it was. His paper, the *Virginia-Pilot*, made headlines of the news. Below the headline were these words: "No Balloon Attached to Aid It."

Other newspaper editors merely laughed. Hadn't they just printed stories saying flight was impossible? Nine days earlier their papers had told about a famous inventor who had tried to fly and failed. Afterward, the scientists had all agreed that a power machine could *never* be made to fly. Why should anyone

believe that two bicycle mechanics had done what a great scientist could not do? It must be a joke.

Wilbur and Orville, of course, kept on flying. During the next few years they made new and better airplanes. They changed the controls so that the pilot could sit up. They made space for a passenger. They added a bigger fuel tank, a stronger landing gear, a more powerful engine.

Several years went by before Orville and Wilbur became famous. Even the United States Government had not been interested in their invention. When foreign governments wanted it, Washington officials finally decided to see what these Wright brothers had done.

"Why didn't we know of this before?" they asked then. "Such a machine will be important to the War Department."

Wilbur and Orville had known all along that their machine was important to science. They knew it would be needed in times of war. And they hoped it would be useful in peacetime, too. They were glad their own country had finally taken an interest in their invention.

They did not know then, of course, that one day the skies would be filled with planes carrying passengers and cargo all over the world. They never dreamed of jetcraft and spaceships.

Orville and Wilbur were the pioneers of the aviation industry, and they stayed in that business for the rest of their lives.

Wilbur lived only a short time longer. He experienced only some of the joys of the fame he and Orville had earned. In the spring of 1912 he died of typhoid fever.

Then Orville worked on alone. It was never the same without Wilbur, and often Orville's thoughts went back to long ago. He remembered the tiny flying toy that Father had brought home from a trip. That had been the real beginning of their invention. He remembered the kite their friends had teased them about. He remembered the printing business and the bicycle shop. All of these had taught them to be good mechanics.

They had done all the important things together—working together, dreaming together.

Orville wished Wilbur could have seen the monument honoring them in Dayton. The last two lines of its inscription said:

"As scientists Wilbur and Orville Wright Discovered the Secret of Flight. As Inventors, Builders and Flyers, they Brought Aviation to the World."

Orville was seventy-six years old when he died in 1948. Before his death a newspaper reporter had asked him: "Mr. Wright, who did the most to invent the airplane—you, or Wilbur?"

Orville smiled. "Neither," he said. "We always worked together. We did our *best* work together."

BIBLIOGRAPHY

Dos Passos, John. *The Big Money*. New York: Random House, 1937.

Fraser, Chelsea. *Famous American Flyers*. New York: Thomas Y. Crowell, 1941.

Freudenthal, E. E. *Flight into History: The Wright Brothers and the Air Age*. Norman, Okla.: University of Oklahoma Press, 1949.

Hylander, C. J. *American Inventors*. New York: The Macmillan Company, 1934.

Kelly, Fred C. *The Wright Brothers*. New York: Harcourt, Brace & World, 1943.

Kelly, Fred C. "Bicycle Craze of Early 1900's," *American Heritage*, December, 1956, pp. 68-73.

Lord, Walter. *The Good Years: From 1900 to the First World War*. New York: Harper & Row, 1960.

McMahon, John R. *The Wright Brothers: Fathers of Flight*. Boston: Little, Brown and Company, 1930.

Meynell, Laurence. *First Men to Fly*. London: T. Werner Laurie Limited, 1955.

Ohio Guide, The. (American Guide Series, Sponsored by The Ohio State Archaeological and Historical Society.) New York: Oxford University Press, 1940.

Powell, William S. "First Flight," *American Heritage*, December, 1953, pp. 40-43.

Wright, Orville. *How We Invented the Airplane.* Edited and with commentary by Fred C. Kelly. New York: David McKay Company, 1953.

Wright, Orville and Wilbur. *Miracle at Kitty Hawk: Letters of Wilbur and Orville Wright.* Edited by Fred C. Kelly. New York: Farrar, Straus & Company, 1951.